GREEK AND ROMAN TOPICS

Food and Drink

KENNETH McLEISH

London
GEORGE ALLEN & UNWIN
Boston   Sydney

First published in 1978

© George Allen & Unwin (Publishers) Ltd 1978

British Library Cataloguing in Publication Data

McLeish, Kenneth
    Food and drink. – (Greek and Roman topics ; 7)
    1. Food – History   2. Beverages – History
    I. Title   II. Series
    641'.0938   DE61.F/   77–30596

    ISBN 0–04–930007–5

Printed in Great Britain
in 11 on 12 point Times
by Cox & Wyman Ltd, London, Fakenham and Reading

Contents

Illustrations

Acknowledgements

I am indebted to the following for permission to reproduce illustrations: British Museum (1, 4, 6, 11, 14, 15, 19, 24, 26, 29). Copenhagen, National Museum (20). Mansell Collection (cover, 2, 3, 5, 16, 17, 18, 22, 25). National Museum of Antiquities, Scotland (28). Réunion des musées nationaux, Paris (10, 13). Staatliche Museen, Berlin (8, 9). United Artists (27).

1   Then and Now

Whether we are rich or poor, famous or ordinary, young or old, a large part of our life is concerned with food and drink. Think about your own family. What kinds of food do you buy, and how much do you spend on it? How much time is spent getting it ready and cooking it? Are meal-times important parts of the day, or do you hurry through them to get to more interesting activities? Anyone who knew the answers to these questions could work out a good deal about the sort of family you are and the sort of life you lead. In the same way, looking at what – and how – people ate and drank in the past is a good way to find out something of what they were really like.

Nowadays food is the basis of a huge, world-wide industry. A large part of a country's trade is in things to eat and drink, or the containers to put them in. Hundreds of thousands of people work in food factories, preparing and packaging millions of items every day. There is a huge advertising industry, spending millions of pounds a year telling us what we ought to like. For twentieth-century man, food and drink are big business.

In ancient Greece and Rome, there was no such food and drink industry. There were farms and shops, warehouses and trading ships, cafés and bars, just like today. But there were no factories, and there was no mass advertising. Packaging and 'convenience' foods were non-existent. Most households prepared everything for themselves: not only the day-to-day meals, but more basic things like butter and cheese, beer and bread, sometimes even flour and cooking oil.

Because there were far fewer mass-produced foods than nowadays, families in the ancient world spent far longer each day preparing food than we do today. Instead of opening a tin of beans, for example, you would have to buy, prepare and cook the beans and sauce yourself – jobs that would take many hours. Even the heating took longer. Today we have instant heat in our gas or electric stoves; the exact heat required can be easily and mechanically regulated. But stoves in the ancient world were usually heated by wood or charcoal. It took time to light them, and a good deal of time and effort to get them to the right heat and keep them there.

How did people manage to do anything else with their time *except* preparing and cooking food? Many of them didn't do much else, but many others had slaves to do most of the work. (You can read about them in detail in the book *Slavery* in this series.) In most Greek towns, there was probably an average of two slaves for every five free people. Later, in the Roman Empire, this proportion was often greater, with averages in some places of as many as three slaves to each free person.

1 Preparing the dough

Rich men had dozens, sometimes hundreds of slaves. Poor families naturally had fewer. But all except the poorest households usually included at least one slave, who worked alongside the mother of the household, or under her supervision, and probably saw to long, boring jobs like tending the stove, milling the flour, preparing the vegetables.

WAS THE FOOD THE SAME AS OURS?

What people eat depends on the part of the world they live in, the climate and the produce the land itself offers. To people outside the frozen North, whale-blubber and seal's blood would seem expensive and revolting foods for breakfast. For Eskimos, hen's eggs and rashers of bacon cooked in a frying-pan would be just as difficult to get, and probably just as revolting. In hot countries – and both Greece and Rome have a warm, sunny climate – people eat less solid food and drink more liquid than people in cold countries. In lush, fertile countries (like Britain) the staple diet often includes cereal crops and flour, and meat and dairy products from grazing animals like cattle. In rugged, mountainous countries (like Greece) some of these things can be scarce and expensive, and the staple diet tends to be based on corn.

If you were transported back from twentieth-century Britain to ancient Greece or Rome, you would not find many of the things we are used to in our diet today, and others would be very different. The Greeks and Romans had no tea, coffee or cocoa. (They drank water, beer or watered wine.) They had no potatoes, no bananas, no oranges. Their milk, cheese and butter were as likely to come from goats or sheep as from cows. There were no mass-produced foods like fish fingers, thin-sliced bread or cornflakes: everything was home-made, or bought from small cook-shops and bakeries the size of corner shops today.

The biggest difference, affecting almost everything cooked, was in sweetening and seasoning. Sugar was unknown in the ancient world. Honey was used instead. If you liked your drink sweetened, you added a spoonful of honey. Cakes and biscuits were sweetened with honey; it was even used in a kind of sweet-and-sour sauce for meat and poultry. For flavouring, far more herbs were used than we have in our kitchens. One writer on cookery mentions over two hundred different ones, of which at least fifty were in everyday use. And the oil used in cooking was usually made from olives – oil that was also used where we would use margarine or butter, in baking, or even simply spread on a slice of bread. Visitors to Spain or the south of France today soon notice the effects on food of olive-oil. In ancient times the oil was even sharper-tasting, and even more widely used.

You will come across many unusual (and sometimes rather nasty-sounding) dishes in this book: squid boiled in its own ink, dormice in honey, wine with goat's cheese, sauce made from salted fish-guts, and many more. But it would be a mistake to think that the diet in ancient

2   A butcher's shop. Many of the items shown are still found in butchers' shops today

Greece and Rome was entirely different from our own. If you went back in time you could live perfectly well, eating many of the ordinary foods of today. In fact the basic diet was hardly different at all: wholemeal bread, eggs, boiled vegetables and salads, fish and shellfish, a little meat, biscuits, cakes and fruit. Goat's-milk cheese (which is still the commonest cheese in Greece) and watered wine would take more getting used to – but they are no stranger to us than Danish blue cheese and tea or coffee would have seemed to the people of Greece and Rome.

HOW DO WE KNOW ABOUT THEIR FOOD?

It is often quite difficult to find out exact details about the ordinary life of the past. This is because few people ever bother to write descriptions or make pictures of everyday activities. No one today writes in a book how people strike matches or open tins – and an archaeologist in the distant future, finding a box of matches or a tin-opener, may well have no idea how they were used, or what for. In the same way, no one in the ancient world bothered to write down how you lit and tended a stove, or served an ordinary meal, or made a bed. Such accounts would be fascinating to us nowadays, but they would hardly have interested the people of the time.

Things are even more complicated for historians today because most of the writing and art of the ancient world was intended for the rich and the middle class. Few ordinary people could read or write, and the main visual art (paintings, statues and carvings) they knew was in great public buildings (temples, theatres, palaces) or street art: announcements and advertisements painted on a whitewashed surface (easy to renew or replace), signs, and carvings of conquest put up by the government. The rich and the middle class weren't very interested in recording the daily life of ordinary people, and so it hardly comes into their art or writings at all.

This means that although we know a lot about cooking and eating habits from Greece and Rome, the descriptions and recipes are very often for large-scale events, expensive meals that would be rare in ordinary houses. (It is as if a historian of the future knew nothing about our food today except Charles Dickens' descriptions of Christmas dinners, a week's menus from the Hilton hotel in London, and accounts of the luxury food served on a great cruise-liner.) The kinds of simple diet described on pages 21 and 49 are never described in art or literature.

How do we know they existed, in that case? In the first place, by using common sense. The huge meals often described in literature – whole roast oxen, peacocks and swans, vintage wines cooled in ice from the Alps, pastries made with exotic Eastern spices like ginger and cinnamon – were far too expensive for ordinary people. And even

3 Trajan's Column, surrounded today by ruined columns and modern buildings. It shows clearly what Roman street art was like: the intention is to impress the onlooker, not to give him information

the rich only had them on special occasions, the ones it was worth writing about and describing in detail. We know that sheep, goats and poultry were kept, that fishing was popular, and that cereals and vegetables were grown. Since these foods don't often appear in accounts of extravagant meals, they must have been eaten at other times: that is, for most of the time by most of the people.

4 Roman spoons, ladles and a cake-tray. These were found by archaeologists at the beginning of this century

The second piece of evidence for ordinary food is rather more exciting. It comes from the 'digs' of archaeologists. Very often, when a new site is uncovered, many indications are found of how and what the people ate. Not only cups and dishes, spoons and knives, but bones and shells, husks of seeds and pits and stones from fruit. Sometimes, as in the palace of Mycenae, storage jars are found with stains or marks in them, showing what they once contained. Some have pictures of the contents on the side (to guide the slaves, who could not read). Most exciting of all, in a few places like Pompeii, where many things are preserved almost exactly as they were, samples of food have been found: ovens full of loaves of bread, frying-pans still on stoves, fruit and nuts in bowls. All the food is calcified (turned to stone and dust), but it is perfectly recognisable. In the gardens of Pompeii, and recently in Britain at Vindolanda (Hadrian's Wall, Northumberland), seeds have been found still alive, which have been planted, have germinated and grown.

Finds like these make it possible to reconstruct what was in the larders and kitchens of the past. We can work out what plants were grown in the kitchen gardens, what foods were sold in the shops, even the diet of soldiers in camp. By taking this knowledge, and adding to it the cooking methods from the rich men's recipes, we can build up a fairly complete picture of the diet of the times – a vital and important part of the picture we have of everyday life.

2 Greek Food

THE LAND AND THE SEA

Greece is a rugged, mountainous country. In ancient times there were few roads, and the rivers were shallow and unsuitable for navigation. Lush, fertile farmland was rare. Most of the fields were small, and the soil was poor and stony, dry in summer and hard to work in winter. The high mountains made land travel difficult over long distances, and the sea was often stormy and hostile to sailors.

These conditions created and controlled the life-style of the people. They lived in small, independent communities, separated from – and often suspicious of – their neighbours. For food, they relied mainly on the produce of their own local area. A few luxuries – and in hard times, necessities – might be imported, but basically people lived on what their own land and sea provided. In some places (fertile Thessaly, for example), the living was reasonable, and towns grew large and prosperous. But elsewhere (Euboea and Megara, for example), conditions sometimes got so bad that food ran out altogether, and boat-loads of colonists set sail to find new homes in more hospitable parts of the world.

'HOMERIC HOSPITALITY'

In the early period of Greek civilisation (up to about 750 BC), most communities were rather like fortified villages: a group of farms clustered round a market-place, and a strongly built central 'citadel' with walls strong enough to withstand the hardest siege. The citadel was often the home of the village chief. He was the most powerful man in the community (sometimes its priest as well), and his authority often depended on owning more land, cattle and slaves than anyone else. We know about these lords from archaeology, from magnificent 'palaces' like those of Pylos, Mycenae or Tiryns. They are also the swaggering lords of Homer's poems: Nestor, Odysseus, Diomedes, Agamemnon.

One of the duties of such a lord – and one of the best ways of proving his superiority – was to provide lavish hospitality for important visitors to the community. Here, for example, is how King Menelaos of Sparta entertains two unknown strangers in Homer's *Odyssey*:

Menelaos gave his orders. His steward hurried through the palace, calling to other faithful servants to go with him. They unyoked the

5 The remains of the palace at Mycenae, perhaps the home of King Agamemnon

sweating horses from the chariot, tethered them in the stables and threw down spelt [a kind of wheat] mixed with white barley for them to feed on. They leaned the chariot up beside the polished gates, and led the visitors into the king's apartments. When the strangers had feasted their eyes on all they saw, they stepped into polished baths, and the slave-girls washed them, rubbed them with olive-oil, and dressed them in woollen tunics and cloaks. Then they ushered them to thrones beside King Menelaos, son of Atreus, himself. An attendant fetched water in a beautiful golden jug, and poured it into a silver basin so that they could wash their hands. She set a polished table beside them, and the dignified housekeeper brought them bread, and served them all kinds of titbits, a choice of all she had. Another slave filled their plates with different kinds of meat, and set golden drinking cups beside them. Red-haired Menelaos beckoned to his guests and said, 'Eat, and welcome. When you've finished your meal, we shall ask who you are.'

(Homer, *Odyssey* 4, l. 37ff)

This showy 'Homeric hospitality' (as it has come to be called) was offered to every important visitor. In Odysseus' own palace, later in the *Odyssey*, even unwelcome guests feast regularly on two kinds of roast meat (goat and pork), bread, sausage, cheese and fruit, washed down with best red wine. Homer never describes the 'titbits' mentioned in the passage above; but they may have included olives, eggs, vegetable salad and savoury dishes made with flour. As the lords ate, servants bustled about. One saw to the table, another brought water, another bread, another wine and meat. (There were no knives and forks on the table. Your food was cut up by the slaves, and you ate mostly with your fingers.)

Of course, food as lavish as this was not for everyone. Homer's poems were written for a rich, noble audience. The food and hospitality he describes are made as impressive as possible, like everything else about his heroes. Even so, archaeological evidence suggests that the life-style he describes was based fairly closely on real life. In Mycenae, for example, huge storage jars for corn, wine, oil and honey have been discovered. The bones from kitchen-dumps show that goats, pigs, sheep and occasionally cattle (perhaps after a sacrifice – see page 32) were eaten. There were bees at Mycenae (there still

6 A vase-picture showing a girl collecting water in an amphora. This water-spring is in a town, and is magnificently surrounded: notice the pillars, the roof and the gargoyle's head on the end of the water-pipe

are), and there was a spring of particularly clear, pure water.

Poor people ate far less meat than the rich. Their staple foods were bread and porridge, with vegetable soup or stew. (Cheese and eggs were the main high-protein foods, but they were not eaten regularly.) Surprisingly, Homer never mentions the eating of fish, even when his characters live on or by the sea. This may show that it was taken for granted, not worth mentioning – or it may show that it was not a food of the rich. Poor people lived on fish, and eating meat was a symbol of wealth.

THE GROWTH OF TRADE

As Greek society developed, this simple diet (still typical of many 'underdeveloped' or 'developing' nations today) began to change. Farming methods improved, and small industries (like pottery or tanning) were begun. Surplus led to trade – and trade led to travel,

7 Greece and the Aegean

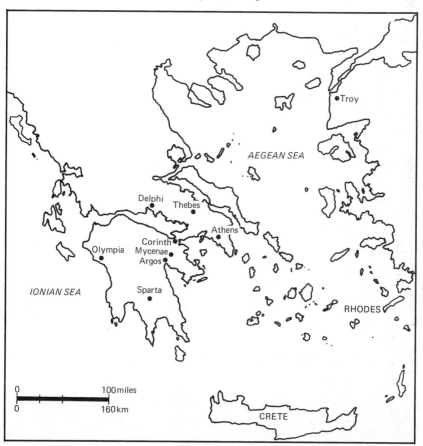

over most of the known world. Many Greek towns grew rich from
travellers. Some, like the island of Rhodes (a safe anchorage half-way
along the corn route from Egypt to the Greek mainland), made their
wealth from the services they offered to traders. Others (like Athens)
became the leaders of political alliances, and accepted yearly tribute
(cash, slaves, trade goods) from their subject-allies. Others again
(like Delphi or Olympia) were the centres of great religious cults,
enriched by the worshippers who flocked to honour their gods. In all
such places, the basic subsistence diet was soon expanded by
imported foods, sometimes necessities brought in to ease local shor-
tages, sometimes exotic and expensive luxuries unheard of in earlier
times.

Many of these imported goods came in the large earthenware jars
called amphoras. Unlike sacks or boxes, these were proof against
damp, as well as pests like mice and rats. They could be packed on
their sides in a ship's hold, wrapped in straw to prevent breakages.
The cargo wasn't a single, dense mass that might shift in a storm and
overturn the ship. It was divided up into a large number of small units
that could be lashed securely down. Amphoras made for more con-
venient handling in the docks and warehouses, too: they were the
Greek world's small-scale, non-mechanical form of container trans-
port.

SHOPPING AND STORAGE

Most of the goods brought in by ship were sold by wholesalers on the
docksides (see page 26). They were then transported overland to
inland areas, or taken to small retail shops in the city centres. In most
Greek towns, shopkeepers selling the same kind of goods kept
together in the same streets. In Athens we know of streets with names
like Potters' Row, Wine Road, Fish Street and Green-vegetable
Lane. As well as specialists like these, there were plenty of open-air
markets, which sold necessities like fresh fish, bread and vegetables,
and every available luxury. A list from Aristophanes' comedy *Peace*
(produced in Athens in 421 BC) tells us the sort of imports his
audience liked. It includes cucumbers, garlic, pomegranates, apples,
geese and ducks from Boeotia, plovers, pigeons, and the most prized
delicacy of all (at least according to Aristophanes): eels from Lake
Copais, sold either alive or preserved in oil like modern pilchards and
sardines (see page 28).

Once you got your shopping home, the hard work began. There
was no problem with fresh food – you bought what you needed, and
ate it straightaway. The markets stocked fish, poultry, meat, vegetables and fruit all the year round, and you bought whatever was in
season. But other things had to be stored, for far longer and in greater
quantities than is normal today. This was partly because all imports

stopped in the autumn. The sea was too treacherous for merchant ships between October and March, and almost no voyages were made. In summer, therefore, when the shops were still full after the harvest and the season's imports, a sensible housewife stocked her larder with enough to see her through all the winter months. She would have large barrels and jars of lentils, grain, wine, oil, dried peas and fruit, and smaller quantities of herbs, spices, onions, garlic, vinegar and honey. (Today we keep perhaps one container of cooking oil at a time – enough for a month or so. In Greek times they had to keep enough for four, five or six months. Multiply this by all the items in a normal store-cupboard, and you can see how the problem grows.)

The second problem came with more perishable foods. The Greeks had no electricity, and therefore no fridges or freezers. Tins and canning had not yet been invented. If they wanted to eat things out of season (cherries in winter, for example), they had to store them in other ways. Many fruits (plums, cherries, figs) were dehydrated in the summer sun, and stored dry. Vegetables were salted, dried or pre-served in olive-oil. Some fruits (apples, pears, quinces) were boiled in honey and preserved in jars. Pickles and chutney were common. If you wanted to keep meat or fish (not often, unless you had an unexpected summer glut on your farm, or a surprise gift of a carcass from a friend), you dried it in strips in the sun, or salted it, or smoked it (like kippers or smoked ham today).

All of these foods required storage space – far more than in modern homes. One of the chief skills of a Greek housewife was in organising her storerooms so that the foods could be properly kept without perishing, and so that they could be reached easily when they were needed. In a book called *Oikonomikos*, or *Managing a Household*, written at the end of the fifth century, a rather houseproud, self-satisfied young nobleman describes in detail how he organised his storage:

When we'd made a list, we began sorting everything out. First we collected together the things used in sacrificing; then we made piles of the women's banqueting-clothes, the men's banqueting-clothes and battledress, blankets for the women's rooms, blankets for the men's, women's shoes and men's shoes. One pile was for weapons, others for items used in spinning, baking, cooking, washing, knead-ing dough and setting the table. All these were further divided into two groups: one of everyday objects, the other, objects for special occasions. We separated items consumed month by month from those that lasted a year – this makes it harder for things to run out unnoticed. When everything was sorted out, we stored each kind of thing in its proper place. We showed the servants where to keep the things they needed each day for baking, cooking, spinning and so on. We told them, 'They're your responsibility: look after them.'

Things needed less often, for special occasions like sacrifices or dinner-parties, we gave into the charge of the housekeeper. We showed her where they were kept, and counted everything, making a written list. Her job was to give them out to any servant who needed them, remember what she'd given out, and when they were returned, put them back in the place she took them from.

(Xenophon, *Oikonomikos* chapter 9)

COOKING AND EATING

That passage (which concerns only clothes and 'hardware', without taking into account any food at all), shows that for a large family, storage was a far more complicated matter than it is today. But when it came to preparing and eating the food, the Greeks spent far less time than we do. For most of the summer months, the weather was too hot for large, heavy meals. But even in winter, no one ate more than one hot meal a day, and some people might eat hot food only once or twice a week. Large quantities of porridge, bread and soup were prepared at once, and they were then eaten cold for the rest of the week. In some households, hot food would only be served on these preparation days; in others, a hot meal might be something you kept for special occasions, after a sacrifice (see page 32), or when you had guests for a dinner-party (see page 37).

In many Greek houses there was no special room used all the time as a kitchen. Greek houses had no running water, no gas or electricity – and this meant that there was no need for fixed sinks, ovens or stoves. Water was fetched by the slaves, and used in jugs and basins; cooking was done on open fires (sometimes outside), or on a kind of

8   A small, portable *eschara* (grill)

9 A *kribanos* (portable clay oven). This one is heated by a wood fire

small portable grill called an *eschara*. Roasting and baking were done in a portable clay oven (called a *kribanos*) about the same size as the ovens on cookers today. The *kribanos* and *eschara* could be set up anywhere, wherever there was a wood or charcoal fire to heat them. Often they were put up in the courtyard of the house, sometimes even outside in the street. If you knew your neighbour was lighting a fire that day, you might ask for a corner of it to do your own cooking. In the same way, small bakers often let out space in their ovens for housewives to bake their own loaves.

Perhaps because of modern entertainments, the average family today has far fewer 'special' meals than were normal in ancient Greece. There, you might be expected to be invited out, or to entertain guests in your own home, as often as two or three times a week if you were rich. At these meals (see Chapter Four), the food would be more lavish and elaborate than usual, and the preparations might take your slaves the entire day. Ordinary meals were very much simpler. Breakfast (*akratismos*) might be no more than bread dipped in wine or olive-oil, and a little fruit. Lunch (*ariston*) might be bread and cheese, with onions, olives or figs. The evening meal (*deipnon* or *dorpon*) might include eggs or fish with vegetables, and cake or fruit to follow. You would drink water, or milk. In cold weather a favourite drink was wine mixed with boiled water and sweetened with honey. Good wine was kept for dinner-parties; but cheaper wine (used one part wine to three parts water) was commonly drunk by everyone in the household, slaves and children included.

3 Farmers, Merchants, Soldiers

Three groups of people are particularly important in the study of Greek food. They are the farmers who produced it, the merchants who used it for trade, and the soldiers and sailors who fought to protect existing food supplies or win new ones. If we look at the way they felt about society, and the way society felt about them, we can find out a great deal about the economic and political life of the time.

FARMERS

The vast majority of people in ancient Greece were personally involved in farming the land. In earlier times (up to about 700 BC), it was not only the ordinary citizens who worked on farms, but also the rich, the people called kings and lords. Except that they owned far more land, these men were farmers just like anyone else. They spent their time protecting the community from invaders and looking after their estates. Centuries later, when Greek civilisation was at its height (about 500–300 BC), farming was still the main occupation of nine-tenths of the people. Although many of them lived in towns, they kept smallholdings in the surrounding countryside, and spent a fair part of each year there, ploughing, sowing and harvesting.

Most of these farms and smallholdings were tiny, and supplied the food needs only of the owner and his family. But there were a few larger estates, supplying vegetables, grain, animals and poultry for the city markets. These estates were sometimes owned by what we would think of as 'part-time farmers'. The playwright Aristophanes is a good example. He had a house in Athens, and spent the six months from October to March in the city, preparing new plays for the spring drama festivals. But every summer he probably went back to his family estates on the island of Aegina, to harvest his produce for the Athenian food markets.

In the book *Work in Ancient Greece and Rome* in this series, you can read in detail about Greek farms. The main crops were corn, olives and grapes (though some places had other specialities: garlic and onions in Megara, for example, or apples in Boeotia). The main animals reared were goats, with occasional sheep and cattle. Songbirds and bees were part of the stock of many Greek farms.

Some Greek city-dwellers regarded farmers and countrymen with scorn. They talked of them as backward, greedy and sly. Others

10 Ploughing

regarded farms as havens of peace and content after the bustle of towns. And peace and content meant plenty of good, simple food. In the words of one of Aristophanes' farmer-heroes, the good things of the countryside included 'figs, myrtles, the sweet blessings of harvest, vintages, violets growing by the well, the olives we love'. In another play, the farmer-hero contrasts his happy country life with the stuck-up wife he married. Here again, the simple life is concerned mainly with food, and town life is showy and artificial:

> Damn the matchmaker who fixed me up with my wife! I lived an ideal life on the farm, shabby, dirty, happy-go-lucky, with bees in my hives, sheep in my folds, olives in my presses. Then I married the stuck-up daughter of Megakles, son of Megakles – me, a yokel, and her, a posh, bitchy, pampered city type. Imagine us at the wedding-feast: me stinking of wine and fig-racks and greasy sheepskins, and her full of perfume and saffron and fancy foreign kisses, parties and banquets and upper-class orgies....
>
> (Aristophanes, *The Clouds* l. 42ff)

Some of the laws passed about farmers and farming show the kind of crops and stock produced, and their importance to the economy and diet of Greece. For example, the only crop produced in enough quantity to be exported from Athens was olives, and there were severe penalties for anyone caught exporting figs, animals or grain. At one time, in the area round Athens, a law was passed setting up a kind

11 These huge bees are from a story in Greek legend. If real bees had ever reached this size, people might have been very glad of laws like the one quoted on this page

of police-force to protect sheep from wolves, and oxen and lambs from rustlers. Other early laws may seem stranger; but they show how vulnerable – and important – some parts of the food supply could be:

The penalty for selling bad fish in the market is banishment.
Bees must be kept at least 100 metres away from your neighbour's
    land.
Stealing figs is a crime punishable by death. (This was later changed to a heavy fine.)
Anyone caught stealing dung will be flogged.
Any slave found drunk while ploughing will be executed.
    (quoted from Potter, *Grecian Antiquities*, published in 1806)

MERCHANTS

At the height of ancient Greek civilisation in the fifth century BC, Athens was a main centre for the trade of the whole Greek world. There were two reasons for this. First, the Athenians had a large number of allies and dependent states, and their trading ships could find friendly ports wherever they went. Second, the Athenian warfleet was the best in Greece, and kept the merchant ships and sea-lanes safe from attack by pirates or enemies.

Because Athenian trade was on such a large scale, the warehouses there were used as a kind of clearing-house, dispatching cargoes of

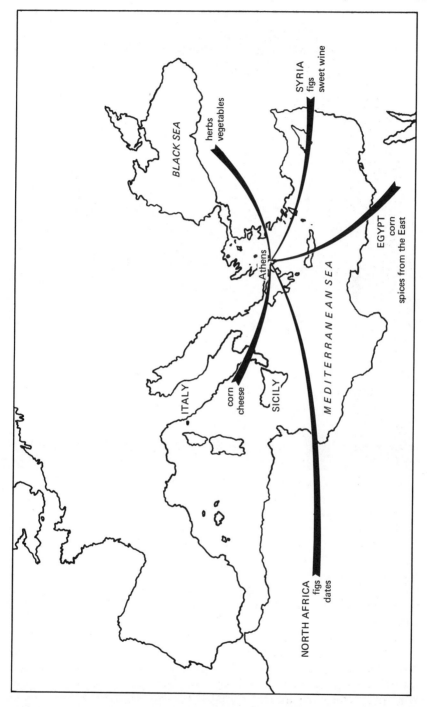

12 Map of the Greek world, showing some of the main food imports reaching Athens in the late fifteenth century BC

essential foods to all parts of Greece. In the halls beside the docks, wholesalers' stalls offered all kinds of luxuries, many of them unobtainable anywhere else in Greece. There were pepper and spices from the Far East; rare wines from Spain in the west and Russia in the east; dates and sweet liqueurs from Syria; figs and nuts from Palestine; fine cheese from Sicily. Many of these goods were resold for export, and loaded on to Athenian trading ships; but certainly some were sold in the open market, and ended up on the tables of ordinary Athenian families.

The most important import of all was corn. The staple foods of most Athenians were bread or porridge, and an average household

13 Women kneading dough. What job do you think the person on the left is doing? (It is something musical.) These women were perhaps neighbours all preparing dough for the same baking. Or they may represent the slaves at a small bakery. The group was probably made as a child's toy

would consume several kilos of grain every week. It has been estimated that an average of 800 small grain-ships landed their cargo at the Piraeus (the port of Athens) every year, unloading 100,000 tons of grain for Athenian use alone. In the sailing months of March to October, that is a hundred ships a month for grain alone – an average of three or four every day.

With such a large-scale and lucrative food trade as this, it is hardly surprising that many crooked merchants indulged in spectacular, complex frauds. Greek courts were full of cases involving insurance firms or private backers who had been cheated of their money. A typical case is the one involving two crooks called Artemon and Apollodoros, in the fourth century. They borrowed money from some Athenian bankers, to finance a trading trip north. They were to take a cargo of 3,000 amphoras of wine to one port, reload there with a cargo of grain, and bring that south. If the merchants disappeared, the wine and grain were to go to the bankers to clear the debt.

Artemon and Apollodoros began by loading only 450 amphoras of wine, instead of the 3,000 contracted for. Then they went to some other bankers, and borrowed still more money on the same security (without telling them of the first loan). They took the wine north, but brought the ship back empty. They landed not in the Piraeus, but at a small inlet appropriately called Thieves' Harbour, and sat tight. Eventually the bankers asked for either their money back or the cargo of corn. Artemon and Apollodoros now announced that their ship had almost sunk in a storm at sea, and they had been forced to throw all the corn overboard. By the law of Athens, if a cargo was lost at sea, no debts could be reclaimed, and no security given. Their bankers took them to court. We have the prosecution speech (by the famous lawyer Demosthenes). But the defence speech and the judgment are missing, and we have no idea whether Artemon and Apollodoros were found innocent or guilty. It is quite likely that they were found innocent – for who can prove or disprove a storm at sea?

WARFARE AND TOWN LIFE

In countries with a mainly rural economy (that is, where the people depend on the land for almost all their day-to-day food), the effects of war are immediate and disastrous. In the last years of the fifth century BC, for example, during the Peloponnesian War (when Athens was fighting many of her neighbouring states), enemy invasions forced most of the farmers around Athens to go inside the city for protection. The overcrowding that followed caused not only political turmoil but also a devastating famine, followed by plague. (You can read about the Peloponnesian War in the book *Sparta* in this series.)

The effects of war on the food supply form the basis of one of Aristophanes' funniest comedies, *The Acharnians* (first produced in Athens in 425 BC). This is partly about politicians and generals (and its humour is as harsh and savage as that of any political satire today). But it also gives a clear picture of what it was like to try to make an honest living – or even just to get enough to eat – under the terrible conditions of war. In one scene a crook from Thebes comes to do business in the market, his bags crammed with black-market goods. The list is exaggerated to make it funny – but we can be sure that it contains either the sort of things Aristophanes' audience liked, or the kind of strange beasts and birds they were being forced to eat because of the war. (The eels at the end are almost a catch-phrase of Aristophanes. They are mentioned in play after play, and perhaps roused a cheer of welcome from the audience.)

Athenian: What have you brought?
Theban: Whatever Boeotia has to offer. Marjoram and penny-
              royal, rushes for mats, lampwicks, ducks, jackdaws,
              wading-birds, coots, wrens, pigeons —
Athenian: Sounds like fowl weather again.
Theban: I've brought geese, hares, foxes, moles, hedgehogs,
              pussy-cats, beavers, martens, terns, Copaic eels —
Athenian: Stop! O bringer of sweet titbits to men, let me speak to the
              eels if you have them ... address them ... face to face....

                    (Aristophanes, *The Acharnians* l. 873ff)

Earlier in the play we meet a more tragic figure: a Megarian, from a
small trading town caught half-way between the two sides in the war.
The area around Megara has been sacked by both armies in turn, and
its famous exports, garlic, salt and onions, have been destroyed. This
Megarian comes to Athens, trying to sell his own daughters for food.
The actual scene is comic and slapstick (he dresses them up as piglets,
a disguise which fools nobody). But its message is a bleak one, and the
scene shows clearly how much a small town depended on its farmland,
and how quickly ruin and destruction followed even a small-scale
enemy attack.

Megarian: Hey! D'you want to buy any pigs?
Athenian: What? Oh, it's a Megarian.
Megarian: We've come to do business.
Athenian: How are things in Megara?
Megarian: We're starving by our firesides.
Athenian: Carving by your firesides? Good fun, if there's a flute-girl
              handy. What else is going on?
Megarian: When I left to come here, the council were just discussing
              the quickest and most painful way to go to hell.
Athenian: You might just be better off there.
Megarian: Huh!
Athenian: Any other news? What's the price of corn?
Megarian: Like the gods – sky-high.
Athenian: Have you brought any salt?
Megarian: You've got your hands on all our salt already.
Athenian: Garlic?
Megarian: What garlic? Every time you invade you root up all the
              shoots ... worse than fieldmice.
Athenian: Well, what *have* you brought?
Megarian: Pigs, for sacrifice.
Athenian: Show me.
Megarian: They're good ones. Feel, if you like. They're good and fat.
Athenian: Whatever's *this*?
Megarian: A pig, of course.

                    (Aristophanes, *The Acharnians* l. 749ff)

SUPPLYING THE TROOPS

The soldiers who dug up the Megarian garlic fields were not indulging in sheer vandalism. Greek soldiers were expected to live off the land through which they travelled. They were usually provided with a basic daily ration of corn, but that was all. They had to depend on whatever the local area could provide for meat, vegetables or other supplies.

In some areas this was easier than in others. During the Trojan War, according to Homer, the area round Troy provided a ten-year living not only for the Trojans themselves, but also for the attacking Greek army. There was hunting in plenty (for deer and wild pigs) in the nearby mountains, and both sides kept large areas of the Trojan Plain as food-farms right through the war. Centuries later (481 BC), King Xerxes of Persia marched on Greece with an army of at least 200,000 men. This huge force had to be fed, and even more difficult, provided with fresh drinking water. For several years before the invasion, Xerxes had to send out advance parties to survey the land and rivers, and set up food-dumps and even farms at regular intervals along the route his army was going to take. His huge invasion fleet (over 1,200 ships) included many merchant vessels carrying basic necessities.

We can get an idea of the numbers of merchant ships needed for an invasion by looking at the figures for the Athenian invasion of Sicily in

14 A huntsman and his dog, returning with their catch (a couple of hares)

15 Clay model of a Roman merchant ship. Most of the space in the wide, shallow vessel is for cargo. The small deck at the back is for the steersman. This boat would be sculled by an oar from the back, or might use a single, central sail

415 BC. There were 60 warships and 40 troop-carriers from Athens, plus 34 fast warships and two large troop-carriers from the allies. These carried an astonishing 28,000 men, ranging from cavalrymen and heavy-armed infantry to the sailors who actually rowed the ships. This force of 136 fighting ships was accompanied by a fleet of 130 official merchant vessels. It carried all the stores, and 2,000–3,000 bakers, butchers, cooks, blacksmiths, armourers, stone-masons and carpenters. In addition, the official fleet was followed by a number of smaller, private vessels whose owners were hoping to find rich pickings either from the expedition itself, or from the enemy once they were defeated.

Most of the merchant ships in such a fleet would be heavier and slower than the sleek warships of the main fighting force. If a fast attack was required, they had to be left behind. And the warships were narrow and streamlined, built for speed. There was no storage space at all on board. It was therefore necessary for them to put into shore every evening, either to look for food, or to eat at the camps established in advance by servants from the merchant ships.

These meal-times were dangerous. The fighting-men in warships were highly trained—for sea-battles. Their training, like their ships, was useless on land, and they were also hampered by the presence of servants and baggage-animals. Sailors on land were a vulnerable target. One Greek admiral noticed how, every evening, his enemy left their ships almost deserted, while the sailors and soldiers went to buy food in the local markets. So he chose that moment to attack their ships – with total success.

If ships were vulnerable through their need to stop for supplies, it was even worse for foot-soldiers on land. They had to walk from one battle to the next, and depended for provisions on camp-followers with wagons and animals, on local supplies, and on goods brought in by sea. The quickest way to defeat an army, therefore, was often not to fight it at all. You began by what are now called 'scorched-earth tactics': burning and destroying all the farmland ahead of your enemy, so that no food was available. Then you defended the inlets on the coast, so that no food could be landed. Lastly, you came up behind the marching army and separated it from the slower and more vulnerable camp-followers. However well-guarded your enemy's provision lines, these guerrilla methods were often far more successful than pitched battles against the main force – and victory over the camp-followers meant that before long the fighting-men would be starved into desertion or surrender.

4 Special Occasions

SACRIFICES

To the Greeks, the gods were very like gigantic men. They had the same passions, pleasures and pastimes – and the same appetites. Normally they ate ambrosia and drank nectar. No mortal could ever taste real ambrosia or nectar – no one knew the recipe. But Greek cooks invented special recipes for mortals to use. You made 'ambrosia' for sacrifices out of fresh water, olive-oil and mixed fresh fruit; 'nectar' was wine sweetened with fermented honey. But when they could get it, the gods were particularly fond of mortal food like meat and wine. The bargain was simple: the gods looked after men and protected them, and in return they were given regular offerings, sometimes praise and worship, sometimes produce or animals.

A normal, everyday offering would consist of a handful of grain or some oil or wine, scattered on the ground with a suitable prayer. Before you drank, you offered a 'libation': you sprinkled a few drops on an altar or on the ground, and named the god in whose honour you were drinking – rather as toasts are sometimes drunk today.

Sometimes, however, it was felt that these everyday offerings were not enough. Perhaps there was a special reason for celebration, or some disaster had to be averted. Sacrifice on a larger scale was needed. The animals for these sacrifices were specially chosen to be as free from blemishes as possible (because the gods liked everything perfect): no marks on the skin, no deformities, no unusually wild behaviour. Such creatures were expensive (a cock might cost the equivalent of a week's wages; a sheep as much as two months'; a bull a whole year's or more). So the sacrifice was a very special event, and its outcome was important. The way the animal died (calmly, without struggling), the appearance of the innards (correct shape and colour), and even the smell of the cooked meat, all had to be exactly right if the god's favour was to be guaranteed.

In Homeric times beasts for sacrifice were often provided from the king's own stock. For him, the sacrifice was an important symbol of wealth and power. For his poorer subjects it meant a holiday, and a rare opportunity to eat fresh meat. Homeric sacrifices were large-scale, public ceremonies, as formal and ritualised as cathedral services today. Here, for example, is King Nestor's sacrifice to the goddess Athene, to ask her to bring good luck:

> He gave his orders, and they all hurried to obey. The heifer came in from the plain, and the goldsmith arrived carrying the bronze tools

of his craft: anvil, hammer and well-made tongs for working the gold. Athene was present, too, to accept the offering. The old warlord Nestor gave the smith gold, and he worked it carefully round the heifer's horns, a glittering sight to delight the goddess's eyes. Two of the young men led the heifer forward by the horns, and another brought water in a flower-patterned bowl, and corn in a basket. A fourth lord stood by, holding a sharp axe to kill the heifer with, and a fifth held a dish to catch its blood.

The old king Nestor made offerings of water and corn, and said a long prayer to Athene; he threw hairs from the heifer's head into the fire, to begin the sacrifice. When the prayers were done and the grain sprinkled, Nestor's son, prince Thrasymedes, went up to the heifer and struck it down: his axe cut the tendons of its neck, and all the palace women raised a cry as it collapsed. The men held its head from the ground while one of the princes cut its throat. Dark blood gushed out, and life left the carcass.

The dead heifer was cut up, and portions were removed from the thighs in the proper manner, and wrapped in a double layer of fat. Slices of raw meat were laid on top, and the old king burnt them on the altar-fire, sprinkling them with red wine. The young men stood by, holding five-pronged skewers in their hands. When the thighs were burnt and they had sampled the inner parts, they cut up the rest of the meat, stuck it on the sharp points of their skewers and roasted it.

(Homer, *Odyssey* 3, l. 430ff)

The people who benefited most from that sacrifice were the king and his noblemen. For them, the sacrifice provided the meat for a lavish banquet: not only diced steak roasted on spits like modern kebabs, but also delicacies like tongue, sausages (made like modern black puddings, of the entrails stuffed with a mixture of grain, fat and blood), and a kind of haggis (the animal's bladder or stomach, filled with grain, blood and chopped-up liver, heart and kidneys). The remaining parts of the animal would be stewed in large cauldrons and served to the poorer people. From a human's point of view, the gods did worst of all: their portion consisted mainly of bones, wrapped in layers of fat and burnt to ashes on the altar-fire.

In later times, Homeric sacrifices like this were reserved for the very richest men, or for state occasions. Ordinary people worked on a much smaller scale: a goat or a sheep was killed, and the family and a few neighbours shared in the feasting afterwards. There were two ways of sacrificing. Either you took your animal to a temple, and the priests sacrificed it for a fee, returning the unused meat to you afterwards. Or else you sacrificed it yourself at home, at the family altar in the courtyard or by the door.

In any one area or street, there would be two or three such domestic

16 These three vases show the kind of expensive pottery rich Greek hosts liked to
have made specially for important dinner-parties. The outside ones are jugs for
wine or water, and the smaller one in the middle would have held olive-oil, or
perhaps perfumed water for hand-washing

sacrifices each month. Everyone would get very excited. The bustle of
preparations was one of the things thought to attract the gods' atten-
tion – and it often attracted undesirable human beings as well. Every
time one of Aristophanes' heroes sacrifices, he is plagued by beggars
of all kinds, from priests and oracle-sellers to out-of-work generals
and politicians. This extract, from the comedy *Peace*, gives a good
idea of the kind of preparations made. It also shows how beggars
arrived unannounced, demanding a share and determined to stay till
they got it:

Slave	What's to be done?
Farmer:	Take the basket and the holy water, and walk round the altar.
Slave:	Right. What next?
Farmer:	Take the torch, and dip it in the water. As for you, sheep – tremble! Now hold out the grain-basket, and give me the basin. Wash your hands, and throw the onlookers some barley.
Slave:	There. What next?
Farmer:	Next, let us pray.

    They pray.

Slave:	Right. Now sacrifice the sheep. Here's the knife.

Farmer:	No, no. Take it inside and do it there. Bring the thighs back outside.

The slave does so.

Slave:	Here you are. You start roasting, while I fetch the entrails and the holy cakes.
Farmer:	Just a minute. Who's this character wearing a laurel wreath?
Slave:	Some kind of prophet, I'd say.
Farmer:	No, it's Hierokles the oracle-seller. Come to object to the sacrifice, I've no doubt.
Slave:	Come for a sniff of the offering, more like.
Priest:	Aha! A sacrifice! To which of the gods? The tail looks very nice. Carry on, then – and don't forget: I get the first slice.

(Aristophanes, *Peace* 1. 956ff)

FAMILY CELEBRATIONS

The important events in a Greek family's life were much the same as in ours: birth, coming-of-age, marriage, death. And in the same way as today, each of them would be marked with a special meal, sometimes a feast or banquet. In addition, the Greeks celebrated other things which we take more for granted: recovery from illness, for example, or a voyage or journey safely made.

Since the gods were thought to be responsible for happiness and good luck, all these celebrations centred on a thanksgiving sacrifice and the feast that followed. Today we often associate a rich,

17 A rich man's drinking-horn, made in the shape of a rearing horse

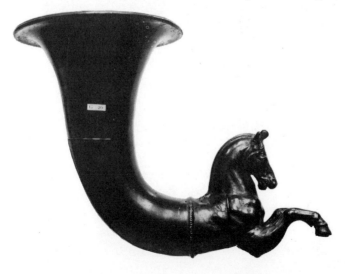

extravagantly decorated fruit-cake with family celebrations like birthdays or weddings; to a Greek family, festive food meant fresh meat. There was another sign of celebration which we might find surprising: the whole family, father, mother and children, ate in the same place at the same table. Normally men rarely ate with their families, but by themselves or with friends, in the part of the house called the *andron* ('men's quarters'). The women and children ate in the *gynaikon* ('women's quarters'). But on special occasions, when there was rich meat from a sacrifice, and neighbours or relatives were invited, the whole family ate together, often in the courtyard or the garden, sometimes even in the street. Professional cooks (called

18 A beautifully decorated large jar for wine or water. (Notice the extra handle on the side, to help lift it.) Only the richest men would be able to afford to have pottery like this specially made

mageiroi) could be hired for the day, and there might be a small cabaret – a flute-girl, a tumbler or a comic actor.

Instead of celebrating birthdays as we do, the Greeks celebrated a child's 'name-day'. This was the tenth day after birth, when it was clear that the child was strong and likely to survive. The child was usually named after his grandfather or his father, but sometimes he would be given a name taken from a trade or profession (such as *Georgos*, 'farmer', or *Myrrhine*, 'seller of myrtle'). A favourite food at name-day celebrations was curd-cheese – perhaps in imitation of the food the baby was likely to eat.

For a boy, the next important celebration was his eighteenth birth-day, when he came of age. After the sacrifice and religious cele-bration, he was declared an adult citizen, and his name was added to the citizen-lists of his local district. Boys swore an interesting oath at this ceremony. It concerns conquest, and loyalty to the city – and the reasons given are entirely to do with farming and food. 'I shall never stop trying to extend the state, so long as there are fields of wheat and barley, vineyards and olive-trees outside its limits.' After this solemn oath a feast was held, probably mainly for the men in the family.

For a girl, the most important family celebration would be her wedding-day. At the age of fourteen or fifteen, she would be intro-duced to her future husband. (Girls had little choice in the matter of whom they married.) Next, the financial details of the marriage were worked out between her father and her bridegroom-to-be. On the wedding-day itself there was no religious service (though there might be a sacrifice). Bride and groom made their marriage promises in front of witnesses, and then spent the day with their relatives and friends, feasting and celebrating. The special wedding foods included toasted cheese (not cheese on toast, but lumps of cheese toasted on spits over the fire), minced meat baked in cabbage leaves, nuts, and small cakes made of flour and honey, often flavoured with sesame.

There was, naturally less celebration at funerals. But just as today, when many people have a special meal after a funeral, so the Greeks met afterwards to eat and drink. Perhaps there was meat from a sacrifice. But the main funeral foods were cheese, olives and tiny, very sweet honey cakes. The mourners drank sharp-tasting wine, some-times mixed with bitter herbs. Often they ate the funeral meal as a kind of picnic beside the funeral pyre (bodies were usually cremated), or beside the family memorial where the ashes were buried. When this happened, they might smash the pots and cups after the meal, and leave the pieces beside the grave.

DINNER-PARTIES

In an age without ready-made entertainments like radio and tele-vision, when there were no newspapers and few books, dinner-parties

19 Vases like this were used at Greek funerals, for oil, perfume, scented water or
    sometimes the ashes of the dead person

were an important leisure activity. They would be common in all classes of society – but especially among the rich. Sometimes there was a single host, and he sent invitations to his friends (often in the form of tiny statuettes of diners). Sometimes several people clubbed together to pay for a particularly lavish meal. Sometimes each guest brought a contribution to the dinner (as we do to a wine-and-cheese or bottle party today). But whatever the organisation, the basic customs were always the same. The guests were always men – if women had parties of their own, which seems likely, no record of them survives at all. There were usually between six and a dozen guests. The food and drink were more lavish and expensive than at ordinary, everyday meals. (Often a dinner-party would follow a sacrifice, to take advantage of both the special occasion and the supply of fresh meat.) And wealthy hosts might even order a set of beautifully decorated dishes and cups (like those in the pictures on pages 34 and 43) to be made specially for the occasion.

There were several ways of catering for a dinner-party. Sometimes your own slaves prepared for it, supervised by your wife. Sometimes you bought the food ready-cooked from a cook-shop. There were many of these, and they either offered you ready-made meals (like a modern take-away), or else cooked your own food according to the menu you gave them. There were a few restaurants, especially fish restaurants in the port of Athens, the Piraeus. But most people seem to have preferred to offer hospitality in their own homes. A favourite way of organising the meal was to hire a professional cook for the day. These men were often experts, specialists in particular kinds of cooking – you might hire a man for his skill with poultry or pastry, for example. They came with their own utensils, and sometimes brought their own trained slaves, and even their own grills and ovens, with them.

The usual kind of dinner-party was in two parts, the *deipnon* or dinner itself, and the *symposion* or drinking-party which followed it. Sometimes guests came to the meal only, and left before the drinking-party; sometimes people arrived after the meal, ready for the drinking-party. Fashionable young men sometimes went on from drinking-party to drinking-party, one after another in the same evening.

20 Not all guests at a drinking-party managed to hold their drink. This vase-picture shows an elegant couch, expensive robes and cushion, and a large, ornate vase. The host at this party would be well-to-do. Notice the garlands of flowers worn by both guest and slave. (This scene was painted on the inside of a drinking-cup – just where you would see it as you drained the last of your wine)

As in a modern dinner-party, the food for the meal could be very elaborately cooked, with as much variety as possible. The first course, like modern titbits or *hors d'oeuvre*, consisted of sharp-tasting snacks to whet the appetite: olives, onions, radishes, pickled thrushes' eggs, nuts, figs and dates in vinegar. The second course was centred on a dish of meat or fish. Squid was a great delicacy, and so were oysters and eels. A meat dish might consist of a goose or duck stuffed with larks and thrushes, a whole roast piglet, a hare stuffed with sausages, or a joint of pork or lamb left to soak in wine, then roasted and served with sauces based on herbs, wine, honey and cream cheese. This course would be accompanied by bread, sometimes dipped in olive-oil flavoured with herbs. The last course was often sweet: a tart of plums or quinces, pears or apples prepared in honey, candied figs and cherries. All through the meal fresh fruits, raisins and nuts were available as side dishes.

When everyone had finished eating, preparations for the drinking-party began. In this scene from a comedy, two slaves are peeping through a curtain, watching the master's guests:

First slave: Have the gentlemen finished eating yet?
Second slave: Almost all of them.
First slave: Good. Take the tables away, quickly. I'll fetch water and soda, so that they can wash their hands.
Second slave: I'll sweep the floor. Then, when I've poured them some wine for libations, I'll fetch the *kottabos*. The flutes should be ready for the girl now; she should be blowing into them to warm them up. Go and sprinkle perfume for the guests: Egyptian violets and irises. Then I'll fetch each banqueter a wreath. Someone mix some fresh wine.
First slave: It's already mixed.
Second slave: Put some incense on the altar.

    Later:

First slave: They've poured the libations, and the drinking's well advanced. They've sung a song, and the *kottabos* is being brought out. The little flute-girl's playing the guests a Carian tune; there was another girl with a triangular lyre, and she sang a bawdy song.
        (Plato Comicus, *The Lakonians* fragment)

(A lyre is a musical instrument, as you can see in the photograph. *Kottabos* was a game of skill. You kept a little wine in the bottom of your cup. When it was your turn, you shook the cup sideways, with a single flick of the wrist. The aim was to throw the wine, in one movement, so that it fell into a metal bowl. If it did. and the bowl

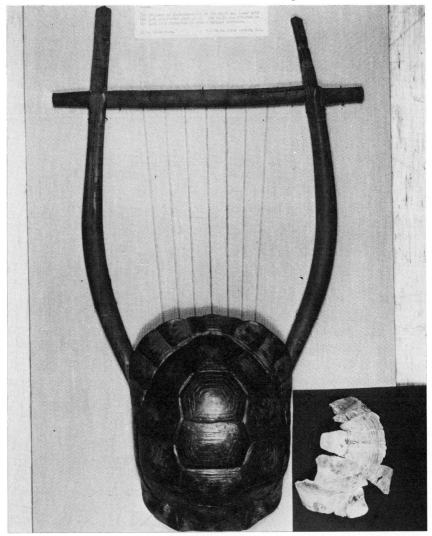

21 This is a rebuilt lyre, now in the British Museum. The lower part, made of horn, has perished: originally it was complete. Each string sounds a different note. Small Irish or Welsh harps today are similar in size and sound

clanged in the right way, you were the winner of that round. If you missed, you paid a forfeit.)

The wine drunk at a drinking-party often came from Asia Minor, or the islands in the Aegean Sea. It was heavier and sweeter than the wine used every day. Wine from Chios, Thasos and Lemnos was thought to be the best. It was mixed with water by the slaves, and served to the guests in elegant drinking-cups, that were to the Greeks what 'best china' is to us. The guests drank toasts, made speeches, sang songs, and sometimes watched a cabaret (like the flute-girl mentioned in the passage above).

5 Roman Food

EATING TO LIVE OR LIVING TO EAT?

Like the Greeks, the vast majority of people in the Roman Empire 'ate to live'. That is, there was little or no fancy cooking for its own sake. The food was simple, and consisted mainly of things necessary for survival. Luxuries were rare treats rather than a basic part of the daily diet. The ordinary foods were much the same as in Greece: mainly bread, dairy products, fruit and vegetables, with meat and fish when they were available. One difference was that many Romans despised porridge as a food. They regarded it as fit only for slaves, or a strange fad enjoyed only by unpredictable foreigners. A slang name for Greeks in Rome was 'porridge-eaters' – and it was a standard joke that they ate nothing else, just as some comedians today imply that Italians eat nothing but spaghetti, or Frenchmen nothing but frogs' legs. Water and wine were the main drinks, and honey was used for sweetening. A wide variety of herbs were used for flavouring. The Romans were also very keen on herbal medicine, which they treated as an important branch of science.

Some early Roman laws show the same anxiety about crops and small farms as the Greek laws quoted on page 24:

> Anyone who burns a building or corn-heap beside a house will be bound, flogged and burnt to death at the stake, provided he committed the crime deliberately; if it was an accident, he must pay for the damage, or if he is too poor, suffer a less severe punishment. Anyone who cuts down someone else's trees deliberately must pay a fine for every tree.
> If your fruit-trees overhang someone else's land, you are allowed to go onto his land to gather the fruit that falls.
>
> (Loeb Library, The Twelve Tables)

The main difference between Roman and Greek cooking becomes obvious if you think of the sheer size of the Roman world, compared with Greece. There was no standard 'Roman' food, eaten everywhere in their vast empire. Instead each country, each region, had its own specialities. The diet of a Roman citizen living in Britain would be quite different from that of Romans in Egypt, for example, while the food eaten in the colonies by the Black Sea, or in central Italy, would be different again. Of course, many of the same things were eaten everywhere in the empire – Roman armies, for example, insisted on having the food they were used to, wherever they went in the world.

22 Rich Romans, like rich people today, collected antiques. These three Greek drinking cups were found in central Italy. They were made in about 550 BC, and 500 years later would be as rare and valuable as Ming vases or Sèvres porcelain today

But in most Roman provinces, the people ate the food they always had eaten, before they became subjects of Rome.

The people who *were* affected by the huge range of foods available were the rulers of the empire: the fantastically rich aristocrats who lived in Rome, and farmed huge areas in Italy or the choicer parts of the empire. They had the money to buy whatever foods they fancied, imported from the ends of the earth. They had often travelled widely in the empire, and seen the exotic foods of far-off lands. Their trading ships travelled everywhere, and brought the luxury foods of the world (and local cooks to prepare them) to kitchens and dining-rooms in Rome.

The diet of rich aristocrats was nothing like that of ordinary people. Their cooks tried endlessly to serve up new kinds of food, or food cooked in new ways. (A typical fad, for example, was to have no food served at your table that looked like itself. Everything had to be disguised: rabbit had to look like poultry, cakes like oysters, fish like fruit, and so on.) You can read about some of the extraordinary dishes of rich aristocrats in the next chapter. But it would be wrong to think that this kind of 'living to eat' is typical of the Romans. It affected only the rich, the people we know most about – perhaps less than one per cent of the population. And even among the rich, many people disapproved of this kind of excess, and preferred a simple diet like that of ordinary people.

FOOD AS A SCIENCE

In Roman times, much of Italy was rich, fertile farmland. The Romans could rely on imports from all over their empire. So there

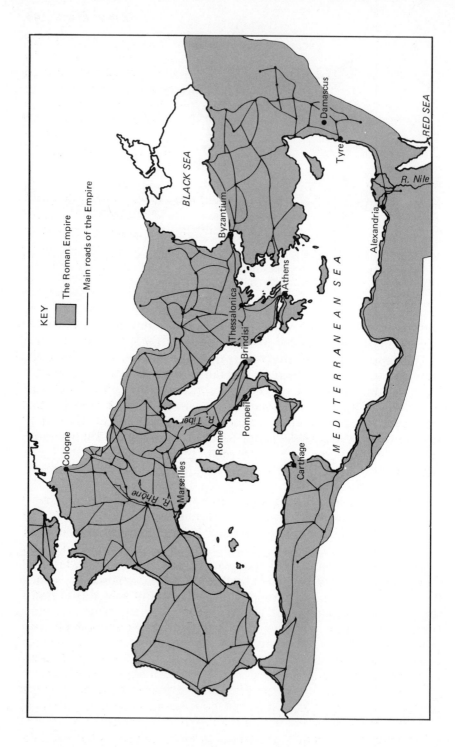

KEY

The Roman Empire

—— Main roads of the Empire

BLACK SEA

RED SEA

Damascus

Tyre

R. Nile

Byzantium

Alexandria

Thessalonica

Athens

Brindisi

MEDITERRANEAN SEA

Cologne

R. Tiber

Pompeii

Rome

Carthage

R. Rhône

Marseilles

23 The Roman Empire

was seldom any real danger of starvation, as there had often been for the Greeks. There were occasional problems with the food supply. In the second century BC, for example, a group of aristocrats hoarded grain in huge warehouses, trying to starve the common people into submission. Then again, a century later, Mediterranean pirates became so numerous that the whole of Rome's sea-trade was, for a short time at least, in serious trouble. But on the whole most people in Italy had enough to eat, and there was a surplus to store in case of a shortage later on.

Perhaps because there was no need to worry about the actual day-to-day supply, the Romans thought far more than the Greeks about other aspects of food. In the Greek world, such matters as farm management, food storage, preparation and cooking were kept very simple. People did what worked, and passed their knowledge on to others, usually by word of mouth. But the Romans gave careful thought to all these matters, conducted experiments and even produced textbooks. Two famous books on farm management (by Cato and Varro) survive. They were written in the second and first centuries BC, and were widely used by the owners of large estates for several hundred years, even forming the basis of farming in some monasteries of the early Middle Ages. They deal with everything: the number of acres a slave can plough in a month, the best length for a slave's tunic, the best soils for growing different crops, the correct seasons for planting and harvesting, whether it is better to grow olives or import them from abroad, how to keep your farm animals – and slaves – contented and producing their best, and so on. The books are full of advice and information. Some of it is quite unexpected. Here, for example, is one writer's view of cabbage. Do you agree?

> Cabbage surpasses all other vegetables. Eat it either cooked or raw. If you eat it raw, sprinkle it with vinegar. It's very good for you, and keeps you regular. Cabbage-water is excellent for all kinds of things. If at a dinner-party you want to eat and drink as much as you like, before dinner eat as much raw cabbage as you want, seasoned with vinegar; then, after the meal, eat half-a-dozen more leaves. This will make you feel as if you've eaten nothing at all, and you'll be able to drink as much as you want.
>
> (Cato, *De Agri Cultura* section 156)

Other writers take a slightly different approach. In the *Natural History* of Pliny the Elder (first century AD) there are long sections on fish, poultry, cattle and game. Pliny's method is to write down every known fact about each of his subjects. His section on pigs covers (1) the best times for breeding, (2) the number of piglets in a litter, (3) when baby pigs should be taken for sacrifice, (4) sows that eat their own offspring, (5) pigs wallowing in mud, (6) curly tails indicating calmness in pigs, (7) pigs recognising the human voice, (8) how to sterilise a sow, (9) fattening pigs for the table, (10) producing *foie gras* from pigs for *pâté*, (11) varieties of pig meat, (12) how to carve pork at table. Another writer, Apicius (first century AD), gave his name to a famous gourmet cookery book. Like Mrs Beeton's book *Household Management* in the nineteenth century, this became a standard work. It was used for at least ten centuries, and was adapted and added to by each new generation of chefs. Some recipes from Apicius are given in Chapter Seven of this book.

24 Bronze cooking utensils from Roman Britain.

Since we no longer farm or cook in the Roman manner, most of these books are useless nowadays as practical guides. But they offer a detailed and fascinating record of what foods were available on Roman tables, and how they were produced and prepared. In this short section from Cato, we learn something about the *vilica* or chief housekeeper of a country estate, and the sort of store-cupboard she was expected to keep:

She must be clean and tidy, and must keep the house clean and tidy. Every night, before going to bed, she must clean out and lay the fire. On the Kalends, the Ides, the Nones and any other holidays, she should hang a garland over the hearth and pray whenever she can to the household god. She must keep a supply of cooked food for you and the servants. She should have plenty of hens and eggs. She should keep stores of dried pears, sorb-apples, figs, raisins, sorb-apples in wine, preserved grapes, pears and quinces. Grapes should be preserved in grape-pulp, and in pots buried in the ground; fresh nuts from Praeneste can also be stored in this way. Quinces from Scantium, as well as wild fruits and the other kinds of fruit normally preserved, should be kept in jars – and she must be careful to stock her store-cupboard with these every year. She must also know how to grind good flour and cornflour.

(Cato, *De Agri Cultura* section 143)

A passage from Varro's book tells us about the incredible variety of plants you might expect to find in a Roman kitchen garden or allotment. Some are familiar to us, and some are strange. They include vines, rushes (for making baskets and mats), brambles, olives, vetch, alfalfa, clover, lupins (for animal food), chick peas, cabbages, flax, beans, sesame, asparagus, walnut bushes, turnips, lentils, onions, garlic, all kinds of herbs and something improbably called 'panic-grass'. In another passage we find fascinating instructions for the storage of fruit:

> Apples keep well in a cool, dry place. Some people lay them on planks, but others prefer straw or even fleeces. Pomegranates have their stalks buried in pots filled with sand; quinces (large and small) are kept in tightly woven baskets; autumn Anician pears are preserved in boiled wine. Some people think that sorb-apples keep best if you quarter them and dry them in the sun (like pears), or leave them just as they are in a dry place. Grape cake should be cut up and kept in mustard, walnuts in sand. Ripe, picked pomegranates also keep well in sand; green ones should be left on the branch, placed in a pot with no bottom, and buried in the ground. Bind the ends of the branches to keep out the air, and when you take the fruit out it will not only be sound, but also larger than it would ever have grown on the tree.
>
> (Varro, *Rerum Rusticarum* chapter 1, section 59)

The interesting thing about the writers who turned food production and consumption into a science is that all of them were wealthy aristocrats, with careers covering government and public life as well as farming. They owned and supervised estates, but they did not actually do the work themselves. They were amateurs, in the same way as Roman philosophers or military historians were often amateurs: they had the money and the leisure to think about their subject, to make experiments, and to write down their conclusions for the guidance of other aristocrats. Many of the wealthiest Roman families made their money in trade, and others in farming (not merely cattle, vines and olives, but exotic specialities like trout, rabbits, mushrooms, dormice and even edible snails). We often think of the Roman aristocrat as a senator in a toga or a military commander on the battlefield. We should add to that the image of a country squire, someone for whom food was not only big business but an important leisure interest as well.

ORDINARY FOOD

It might seem at first that all those aristocratic activities had little or nothing to do with ordinary people, and that the food of the great mass of Romans was nothing like that of the rich minority. Certainly it

25 Rich men liked to remind themselves of hunting and farming, even in the decoration of their homes. This mosaic floor shows a boar hunt in progress

is true that only a small group of Romans had the time and money to spend on fancy dishes like the ones in Apicius' recipe book. Most ordinary people ate plain, simple food; rich recipes were kept for special occasions, as they are for most people today.

Nevertheless, the wealthy Romans were crucial to the everyday life of ordinary people. This had never happened before, in Greece, Egypt, or any other ancient civilisation. First, they controlled and ran trade, farming, marketing and banking. They were often the landlords of streets of small market-stalls and food shops. Their knowledge and experience were put to use not only in providing their own food, but also in supervising the food supply of almost every citizen.

Second, Roman civilisation worked on an elaborate system called 'patronage'. Every rich man gave help and support to a group of poorer, less powerful citizens. In Rome, in particular, the common people often depended for survival on a dole of imported corn, given out by the aristocrats who governed the city. In fact, one writer in the first century AD wrote scornfully that the common people were only ever interested in two things: bread and circuses (that is, free food and free entertainment). The patron often lived as the squire of a small town or country area, and helped it directly with cash, buildings (such as grain warehouses) and the direction of farming and trade. Even in cities, a rich man would have a large number of dependants: his more well-to-do 'clients' (a group of supporters who visited him regularly, and helped him in business or politics, in exchange for favours); and his tenants, freedmen and slaves who might manage warehouses and shops in the quarter where he lived.

In this way, ideas discovered and used first of all by the rich gradually worked their way through to the daily life of every citizen. The farms of Italy produced more than their owners needed, and that surplus filled the town markets. The new science of animal and plant breeding (where the 'stock' is improved to produce more meat on an animal, or a more fruitful and disease-proof plant), guaranteed a higher standard of food for everyone, regardless of status. The all-important art of food storage, first developed on the huge estates of the aristocrats, was scaled down and adapted to suit the needs of ordinary men. Even the diet and eating habits of the rich eventually affected everyone. Two good examples are the way in which bread replaced porridge as a staple food, and the growing popularity of beer, which began as a luxury drink imported from abroad, but soon became as common as wine, water or fruit juice.

For everyone, the first meal of the day was breakfast, or *ientaculum*. You ate it sometimes as you dressed, sometimes on your way to work, sometimes as you began work. It was such a slight affair that there was no need to set a table and spend time simply in eating. Some people (on the advice of doctors or slimming consultants – the Romans were as addicted to weight control as we are today) took nothing but a glass of water or a cup of light wine. Others had bread, with cheese or a little fruit. One writer tells us of schoolboys calling at the pastry shop on their way to school, munching their *ientaculum* fresh from the oven.

The meal for the middle of the day was lunch, or *prandium*. This, too, was light, usually cold, and hardly worth setting a table for. Once again bread was the main part, perhaps with some cold meat or cheese, accompanied by olives, pickles or nuts, and followed by fresh fruit. With it you drank water, beer or sweet wine.

The main meal of the day was dinner, or *cena*, and was eaten round about dusk. Men, women and children all ate together, unless the father of the family was giving a dinner for his friends. It was considered polite for a man to eat lying on his side, resting on one elbow. The better-off had special dining-rooms in their houses, with couches (*triclinia*) sometimes built into the walls in a special horseshoe arrangement. But most people would simply arrange portable couches in the required number and position, or eat at tables set up in the courtyard or garden, as people did in Greece. (Remember that the climate of Greece and Italy is much warmer than ours. Today, people in those countries often eat on a veranda, or out of doors, in the cool of the evening.)

The evening meal was more elaborate than any of the others. The basis was probably meat or fish, with vegetables. A trayful of cold snacks was a favourite dish: egg-yolks in cream sauce, prawns and other small sea-creatures, olives, pickled nuts, mushrooms, sometimes balls of minced liver, sausages and, on special occasions, dormice, small songbirds or snails. To follow you would have fruit, either fresh or preserved in wine or honey. There would also be cakes and pastries, sweetened with honey and flavoured with fruit, dried fruit or spices and flower petals. The drink was watered wine. In cold weather hot water was added to the wine, and the drink, called *mulsum*, was fortified with a spoonful of honey or sweet fig-paste.

Many Romans liked their food highly spiced and flavoured, far more than most people in this country today. They imported many Eastern spices from Egypt (where the camel-trains arrived from Arabia and India), and black pepper was particularly highly prized. The herb garden gave them a huge variety of plants (often added to recipes for their medicinal powers as well as their flavour). We would recognise such things as garlic, bay leaves and mint, but perhaps be surprised by asafoetida or 'rocket'. And above all, Roman cookery involved a wide range of highly flavoured gravies and sauces.

The most common sauce (as frequently used in Roman cooking as stock-cubes or gravy browning today) was called *garum* or *liquamen*. It was made from salted fish (see page 58), and was very strong indeed (like our Worcester sauce or sharp brown sauce). It was used in sweet recipes as well as sour, and seems to have been added to Roman cooking wherever we would add a pinch of salt. Another common sauce was *defrutum*. This was wine boiled down until most of the liquid evaporated, leaving a quite thick stock often added to sweet dishes (see page 58). All sauces could be kept for years in corked amphoras, and in fact there were 'vintages' of sauces, just as there are of wines. The most pungent sauce of all was vintage *liquamen*, called *allec*. If, after some years, the jar was uncorked and the mixture smelled superb, it was highly prized, and used for the most expensive cookery. If it had gone bad, it could still be used for rough cooking (such as the porridge served to slaves on farms).

Like the Greeks, the Romans were lovers of fine wines. Many Greek wines were imported into Rome much as good French wines travel the world today. There were exotic wines from other parts of the empire, too: sweet wines from the Black Sea, fig and date wine from Egypt, raisin wine from Spain and North Africa. But the commonest wines were those from Italy itself. There were over eighty different table wines, each from a different district. The right soil and the right weather conditions were carefully studied, and vine-growing was a complicated and exact science. The Romans thought that wines from northern Italy were the best, equal to the finest imported Greek wines. The wines from the area of Mount Vesuvius were popular, and were exported widely throughout the empire. But just like today, few people could often afford expensive, vintage wines. Most regularly drank non-vintage, local wine, shipped to the market in bulk and sold by the jugful from large vats in the local wine-shops.

6 High Society

Roman literature tells us a great deal about high-society banquets, dining-rooms and table-manners. Most rich Romans probably spent many hours at banquets, official or private. What they ate, where it came from and how it was prepared were important matters. Even more than today, what is called 'connoisseurship' in food and wine (knowledge, judgement and good taste) were necessary for any young man destined for public life.

For the connoisseur, the chief meal of the day was the *cena*. In the best houses, the diners wore special evening dress (as some people do today): a tunic and toga of light muslin, sometimes changed between courses. They reclined on couches, and ate with the very tips of their fingers. They used small knives for fruit and cakes, spoons for sauces and cream, and tiny spears for getting snails and shellfish out of their shells. Toothpicks were also provided, sometimes made of silver to match the dishes and salt-cellars on the table.

The place you were given on the dining-couch (most couches were for three guests), the way you wore your garland of flowers and your evening clothes, and even the way you picked up your food or held your wine-cup, were matters of importance, with proper rules and customs. (There are 'rules' about polite eating today, of course. For example, you shouldn't eat peas with a knife, or drink your soup noisily; wine should be drunk slowly, not at a single gulp; there is a 'right' way of folding and placing your napkin, and so on.) Two differences between Roman good manners and ours were that it was regarded as 'best behaviour' (a compliment to the cooking) if you belched as you finished eating; and the guests sometimes took their own napkins to the dinner, and filled them with titbits to take home (again, a compliment to the cooking).

After the eating was over, the banquet often moved to a second stage, the *comissatio*. This was a drinking-party, very like the Greek *symposion*. Choice wines were served, and the guests enjoyed conversation, sang songs or recited verses, and watched cabaret – dancers, comedians, singers or actors. At the most serious, official banquets the guests might discuss matters of trade or state; but the Romans generally liked to get their business matters settled during the day, and to keep the conversation light-hearted and easy. (Even so, a rose was pinned overhead, to remind them of the ancient tradition at dinner-parties, that anything said *sub rosa*, 'under the rose', was meant for the guests' ears only, and should go no further.)

Basically, a *cena* or dinner consisted of three courses. First came the *gustatio* (appetisers and *hors d'oeuvre*). This was followed by the *primae mensae* ('first dishes'): fish, poultry and meat, served with vegetables and bread. The last course, *secundae mensae*, consisted of sweet dishes: fruit, pastry and cakes. Each of these courses could be subdivided into two or three smaller ones. At really big banquets there were often seven courses: the *gustatio*, three courses of fish and poultry, two courses of roast and finally the *secundae mensae*.

We can see the kind of dinner-party given by men of good taste in a meal served to seven friends by the poet Martial (first century AD). He moved among the upper class, but was not a great landowner. He earned enough to live well from his poetry, but was by no means a rich man. This meal is probably very typical of the sort of party a well-to-do Roman might give or attend four or five times a month. The *gustatio* consisted of sliced hard-boiled eggs, small fish poached with rue, and sow's-belly (a favourite Roman delicacy) stewed in fish stock. It was served with a salad of green vegetables: lettuce, leeks and mallow, sprinkled with mint dressing. The main course (for eight people, don't forget) consisted of a roast kid, sausages, a chicken and some cold ham, served with sprouts and beans. The last course consisted simply of apples. One kind of wine was served with the meal, a 'good year' but nothing like the real vintage wines (sometimes over a hundred years old) favoured by extravagant hosts.

This is quite an expensive meal, out of the range of many ordinary people. But it is hardly grotesque or wildly extravagant. Simple, good food like this was particularly favoured by the many Roman aristocrats who tried to follow the principles of philosophy – principles like 'Nothing in excess', 'Know yourself' or 'Neither too much nor too little: just enough'.

BAD TASTE

But philosophical rules like these were not to everyone's taste. For some rich men, the purpose of their dinner-parties was not so much to satisfy and delight their guests, as to stun them with the sheer wealth and extravagance of the host. Some of these meals had as many as twenty or thirty courses. They went on all night, and the guests had to stagger out into the street or garden (or to a special room suitably called the *vomitorium*) to get rid of one lot of food and make room for the next. Scented water and rose petals were sometimes sprinkled on the guests from the ceiling, and the banqueters were entertained by dancing-girls, dance-bands and whole circuses of tumblers, sword-swallowers, midgets and acrobats. The phrase 'a Roman orgy' has passed into history. It means a ludicrous, sordidly extravagant mixture of expensive food, drunkenness and sex. Perhaps there were actually very few such occasions in Rome itself. But the disapproving Christians of the first few centuries AD, and a number of pagan writers

26 An official portrait of Nero – perhaps flattering

who liked to mock the rulers of Rome, made the most of all the sordid details, as if this was the way in which the masters of the world always behaved.

The most famous account of this sort of banquet is called 'Cena Trimalchionis' ('Trimalchio's Dinner-party'). It is one section of a comic novel called *Satyricon* (*Bits and Pieces*), written by Petronius in the first century AD. Petronius may have been one of Nero's courtiers, and some people identify the fat, tasteless multi-millionaire Trimalchio with the emperor Nero himself. Petronius' book is fiction – but it gives a clear idea of the sort of bad taste that made his aristocratic audience laugh.

At Trimalchio's dinner-party, each of the three basic courses was subdivided into several smaller ones. The meal began with the *gustatio*, very elegantly presented:

A donkey made of Corinthian bronze was brought in on a serving-trolley. On its back was a pair of panniers containing olives (green on one side, black on the other). Flanking it on either side were two side dishes, engraved on their rims with Trimalchio's name and the weight of the silver. Small dishes shaped like bridges were soldered to them, and held dormice dipped in honey and coated with poppy seeds. There were hot sausages served on a silver grill, under which damsons and red pomegranate seeds had been placed (to give the effect of glowing charcoal).

(Petronius, *Satyricon* section 32)

The second part of the *gustatio* followed: imitation peahen's eggs modelled in pastry (weighing 300 grammes each), one for each guest. When they were opened, baked orioles (small songbirds) were discovered, as though waiting to be hatched.

The main course was a whole roast sow, stuffed with sausages and black puddings. But before it there was served a really fascinating dish. Both the food involved, and the way in which it was presented, are examples of the Roman idea of bad taste at its most involved and extraordinary:

A round tray was divided into the twelve signs of the zodiac. On each sign the chef had placed suitable food. On Aries were chick peas of the kind called 'Rams'; on Taurus slices of beefsteak; on Gemini testicles and kidneys; on Cancer a crab-shaped crown of flowers; on Leo an African fig; on Virgo virgin sow's-belly; on Libra a pair of scales with a roll in one pan and a cake in the other; on Scorpio a small crayfish; on Sagittarius a bull's-eye; on Capricorn a lobster; on Aquarius a goose; and on Pisces two mullets. The centre-piece was a honeycomb laid over a piece of turf with the green grass still growing. An Egyptian slave-boy (from the grain-country) took bread round in a silver dish, bawling a tune from the musical 'Asafoetida' as he went.

We were hardly eager to start on this miserable food. But Trimalchio said, 'Come on, eat up! That's what food's for!' As he spoke, four slaves pranced in, in time to the orchestra, and lifted off the whole top part of the dish. We saw underneath, in a second dish, plump chickens, sow's-belly, and in the centre a hare got up with wings to look like Pegasus. Four little statues of Marsyas (one at each corner) caught our eyes: from their wine-skins a spicy gravy poured out over some fish, which seemed to be swimming in the current. The slaves began to applaud, and we joined in; then, laughing, we prepared to enjoy the delights before us.

(Petronius, *Satyricon* section 35ff)

27 A scene from a modern film version of Petronius' *Satyricon*. In the scented smoke from incense-burners, the guests at Trimalchio's dinner-party enjoy themselves. Trimalchio, attended by the two slaves, is in the centre of the picture

The guests are later offered many sweet pastries and cakes, and all kinds of fresh fruit. With the meal wine is served from cobwebby glass bottles labelled 'Genuine Falernian. Guaranteed one hundred years old'. There are long gaps between the courses, filled with drunken conversation, extraordinary cabaret acts from Trimalchio's slaves, and a game of draughts played with gold and silver coins. The entertainment at the drinking-party afterwards includes stories of ghosts and werewolves, and the reading of Trimalchio's will.

'Trimalchio's Dinner-party' is the longest and most absurd account of a Roman banquet to come down to us. But there are many shorter ones, by such writers as Cicero, Horace, Juvenal, Pliny the Younger and Martial. Banquets given by the emperors are recounted by historians like Tacitus and gossip-writers like Suetonius. Where the writers approve of their subjects, the meals described are simple and elegant, like Martial's dinner described above. Where they disapprove, the meals are ludicrous and tasteless in the style of Trimalchio. This may simply indicate that what a writer likes he calls good taste, and what he doesn't like he calls bad taste. But it may also show something of the kind of moderate eating habits actually preferred by the Romans, and the kind of *luxuria* (showy extravagance) that they thought should be avoided at all costs.

7 Utensils, Methods, Recipes

UTENSILS AND METHODS

Many of the utensils and methods used by the Greeks and Romans were almost identical to those of today. Spoons, ladles, knives, choppers, bowls, sieves, dishes and pots were exactly the same. Saucepans weren't used: instead, pots and pans (of metal or earthenware) were stood on grids and tripods on the charcoal, and cauldrons were hung on hooks over the flames of the cooking-fire. Cake dishes and baking trays were the same as ours. Serving dishes and plates, too, were similar – though the designs of good-quality dishes and pots

28 Bronze cooking pots, with a tripod and gridiron

were quite unlike those of today. Glass bottles were expensive, and earthenware jars were commonly used instead. Instead of cups and mugs, the Greeks and Romans used all kinds of differently shaped goblets and drinking vessels, often beautifully decorated.

A key piece of equipment for an ancient cook, not much used today, was a pestle and mortar. The mortar was a shallow bowl, usually made of wood or earthenware, and about the size of a large ashtray or small pudding basin. The pestle was a rod, usually made of wood, about 3 centimetres thick and 15–20 centimetres long. Its end was blunt and rounded, sometimes hardened with a tip of metal or earthenware. The pestle and mortar were used for grinding and crushing: not only things like pepper-corns and garlic cloves, but vegetables, fish and meat as well. Seeds and nuts were pounded in the mortar, and the Greeks and Romans also used the roasted pips and stones of fruit, pine-kernels and even ground-up charcoal, added in pinches to give an 'edge' to the flavour of both food and wine. Today we buy things like ginger, mustard and cornflour already prepared, dried and ground into powder. A cook in the ancient world would grow or buy the ingredients, dry them and grind them himself with the pestle and mortar.

If you have ever tried cooking on an open fire or a barbecue, you will know that the greatest problem is keeping the temperature exactly right: as the fuel (wood or charcoal) burns, the heat increases or decreases suddenly and rapidly. To get precisely the right temperature, and keep it for the whole cooking time, is difficult – and something you can hardly manage yourself at the same time as seeing to the actual cooking. In Greece and Rome there were two ways of getting, and keeping, the heat exactly right. First, there was a slave whose special job was to see to the fire. He kept a supply of fuel handy, and water to slow the fire down if it grew too hot. He had bellows to blow it up, or to direct the air-flow to a particular part of the grill to make it hotter than the rest. The second method of controlling the temperature of your cooking was to use a large number of pan-stands of different sizes, tripods and hooks. You kept the heat of the fire more or less constant, and pans needing most heat were put on the lowest stands, so that they were nearest the fire. Pans

29 Ladles, strainers and spoons from a Roman kitchen

needing less heat, for slow cooking, were put on high tripods, or hung on hooks above the fire.

Many of the cooking methods of the ancient world are still used today. In the ovens food could be roasted, baked and kept hot. *Bain-marie* cooking (putting the food in a covered pan, and placing that pan in a larger pan of hot water) was frequently used. On top of the fire or stove food could be fried (both shallow frying, which we use for bacon, and deep frying, which we use for chips). Food was also boiled and stewed (in pans on stands or cauldrons on hooks), and grilled on spits. Some cooks had chimneys and flues by their stoves, and could hang cheeses, game, poultry and meat there to be smoked. Bottling and preserving were very common – for meat as well as vegetables and fruit. These three short recipes show different methods of preserving meat: hanging, pickling and salting (and how to get rid of the salty taste afterwards).

Keeping meat fresh without salting: Cover the meat all over with honey, and place in a pan. Hang the pan up in the store-cupboard. This method works well in winter, but in summer you should use the meat within a few days. The method can be used with cooked meat as well as raw.

Keeping pork or beef skin and cooked pig's trotters: Cover in a mixture of pounded mustard, vinegar, salt and honey. Store and use as required. The result is delicious.

Salting meat: Leave the meat to soak in a strong solution of salt-and-water for seven, fourteen or twenty days. It can then be kept in the water until required, or hung in the usual way. *Getting the salt out:* cook the meat twice, boiling it first in milk and then in fresh water.

(Apicius book 1, sections 7 and 8)

TWO VITAL INGREDIENTS: *DEFRUTUM* AND *GARUM*

Defrutum was used by both Greeks and Romans, in sweet dishes and sour, meat and fish as well as pastry. It was also the basis for a number of made-up drinks. To make it you simply boil wine until two-thirds of it has evaporated. What is left can be used as it is, or thickened with flour (or paste made from figs or dates) and sweetened with honey. Sometimes whole fruit (plums, quinces, cherries) were boiled in the wine, to alter the flavour. Some cooks also believed that you could change the flavour by using a particular wood (fig, olive, apple) on the cooking fire used to heat the pan.

Garum was a Roman speciality, used in every kind of dish, from stewed fruit and sweet pastry to the most pungent of stews. It was also sometimes diluted with water or wine, to make a refreshing drink. There were two basic ways of making it. The long way was to take a mixture of small fish (sprats, anchovies or small red mullet) and the entrails of larger fish. You put them in a tub with a great deal of salt, and left it in the sun. You had to shake the mixture, or stir it, frequently. The process took two to three months, so it was best to make a lot at once. When the process was complete, you drained off the liquid: that was *garum*. A quicker, easier way was to prepare a pan of salt-and-water (you could test to see that there was enough salt by putting in an egg in its shell – if it floated, the mixture was right). When it was ready, you added the fish and fish-guts, together with some herbs (origano was thought to be very good), and boiled the whole thing in the same way as *defrutum*, until two-thirds of the liquid evaporated. Sometimes you added wine at the boiling stage. You left the liquid to cool, strained it two or three times, and stored it in sealed jars.

SOME RECIPES

Most of these recipes are translated or adapted from the cookery book of Apicius (who collected dishes from both Greek and Roman kitchens). Some are based on ideas from other writers: Aristophanes, Cato, Pliny the Elder, the physician Galen. Some have been chosen because they give an idea of what Greek and Roman cooking was like at its most typical; others are easy dishes you may like to try for yourself. Ancient recipes never give quantities or proper timings, and it would be a good idea to discuss your chosen recipe with an experienced cook before you begin getting the ingredients together. Then you'll find out exactly what's going to be required, and you may also get some ideas on alternatives for unusual ingredients like asafoetida or rue. (You do not need to use *defrutum* or *garum*. Replace *defrutum* with very sweet cooking sherry; for *garum* use extra salt and a little cod-liver oil. You can leave both out if you prefer, but the dish will taste slightly different.)

Dishes for the first course

Sausages
Chop the meat up small, and mix thoroughly with breadcrumbs that have been steeped in wine overnight. Add ground pepper, *garum* and (optional) myrtle berries with the seeds removed. Make into balls and place in sausage-skins, adding also ground pine-kernels and whole pepper-corns. To cook: simmer gently in a mixture of *defrutum* and water.

Pease-pudding salad
Soak dried peas overnight, in wine or water. Do not drain. Bring the mixture to the boil, cook, stir, cool. Stir thoroughly when cold. Add a finely chopped raw onion and the grated white of a hard-boiled egg.

Olive-oil, salt and vinegar can be added to taste. Place in a serving dish, sieve hard-boiled egg-yolk over the top, and sprinkle with a little olive-oil.

Boiled eggs
Soft-boil and shell the eggs. Serve in a dish, with a sauce made either of *garum*, olive-oil and wine or *garum*, pepper and asafoetida.

Soft-boiled eggs can also be beaten with pine-kernels (soaked overnight), and the mixture blended with pepper, lovage, honey, vinegar and a little *garum*.

Meat and fish

Stew
Cut meat into small pieces, and cook in plenty of *garum*. Sprinkle with pepper and serve.

Roast
Place meat in an oven-tin, and sprinkle with plenty of salt. Roast in the oven. For the last half-hour, baste with plenty of honey. (Use less salt for ham than for other meats.)

Ham in pastry
Boil the ham until it is cooked, in water with plenty of dried figs and three bay leaves. Cool it and skin it. Cut cross-shapes in the fat, and fill them with honey. Make a pastry cover of wholemeal flour and olive-oil, and wrap all round the ham. Bake in the oven for an hour, or until the pastry shell is thoroughly cooked.

Kidneys
Cut open and stuff with a mixture of ground pepper, pine-kernels, coriander and fennel. Close, sew up and cover with sausage-skin or a basting of dripping. Brown in a frying-pan in a mixture of *garum* and olive-oil. Grill (or roast in the oven).

Dormice
Gut and clean. Stuff with minced pork, minced dormouse, pepper, pine-kernels, asafoetida and *garum*. Sew up, place on a flat dish and roast. (Note: this method can also be used for small birds. The flavour is sometimes improved if the flesh is soaked in wine overnight.)

Squid
Cook whole in a frying-pan, in a mixture of pepper, rue, a little honey, *garum*, a little *defrutum* and olive-oil. Serve in a sauce made from pepper, lovage, coriander, celery seed, egg-yolk, honey, vinegar, *garum*, wine and olive-oil, thickened with cornflour.

Fried fish with sauce
Clean, salt and fry the fish. Mix ground pepper, cumin, coriander, asafoetida, origano and rue. Moisten with vinegar, and add date-paste, honey, *defrutum*, olive-oil and *garum*. Mix well, and bring to the boil in a pan. When the sauce is boiling, pour it over the hot fried fish, sprinkle with pepper, and serve.

Patina
Chop finely together cooked sow's-belly or pork, fillets of fish and chicken. Beat eggs in a pan with pepper, lovage and a little *garum*, wine or *defrutum* and olive-oil. Bring this egg mixture to the boil, and allow to thicken a little. You will also need ready-cooked cakes of wholewheat flour and olive-oil, fried or baked in the oven. To serve: place a cake in the bottom of the dish, cover with a layer of chopped meat, and a layer of the egg mixture. Add another cake, more meat, more mixture, and continue until the dish is full. Sprinkle with pepper and serve.

Sweet dishes

Bread pudding
Take the crust from a wholewheat loaf. Break the bread into fairly large chunks, and soak thoroughly in milk. Fry in olive-oil till brown. Serve covered with melted honey.

Egg pudding
Mix four eggs with half-a-pint of milk and a little olive-oil. Put some oil into a deep frying-pan, make it sizzling hot, and pour in the egg mixture. When it is cooked, serve in a dish with honey and a light sprinkling of pepper.

Honey cakes
Make a paste of wholewheat flour, honey and a little olive-oil. Cut into rounds, and either fry in a hot pan or bake in the oven. (Note: this recipe can be adapted to make cheese cakes. Either add freshly grated cheese to the above ingredients, or replace the honey with grated cheese.)

Further Study

READING (NOTES FOR THE TEACHER)

The two most important ancient authorities are Athenaeus and Apicius. Athenaeus is published (in eight volumes) in the Loeb Library. The best version of Apicius is in *The Roman Cookery Book* by Flower and Rosenbaum (Harrap 1958). This not only gives the Latin text and a clear translation, but is also full of hints and comments on how the recipes can be repeated in modern kitchens.

Other relevant ancient authors are first, Cato, Varro and Pliny the Elder (all Loeb Library). Many of the epigrams of Martial (Loeb Library) concern food. Petronius' *Satyricon* offers not only the 'Cena Trimalchionis', but an amusing account of other types of Roman *luxuria*. The best translation is perhaps by William Arrowsmith (University of Michigan Press and Mentor Books 1959). Homer, Aristophanes, Plautus and Juvenal give occasional glimpses of food and eating habits. Complete versions are available in the Penguin Classics series, and shortened versions are available from several publishers. Aristophanes' *Acharnians* is in *Four Greek Plays* by Kenneth McLeish (Longman 1964), a shortened version made especially for schools.

Modern books relevant for projects include the other books in this series, and the *Aspects of Greek and Roman Life* series published by Longman. There are chapters on eating and drinking in Carcopino's *Daily Life in Ancient Rome* (Penguin 1970) and Paoli's *Rome, its people, life and customs* (Longman 1963). Ehrenberg's *The People of Aristophanes* (Blackwell, Oxford, 1943) is full of information about Greek farming, food and everyday life. Accounts of excavations (for example at Pompeii, Herculaneum, Fishbourne and Vindolanda) often contain interesting sections about food.

More general themes and topics mentioned in the book may be pursued as follows: for the farmer-heroes of Old Comedy, the best plays are Aristophanes' *Acharnians* and *Peace*, and Menander's *Bad-Tempered Man*. Xerxes' invasion of Greece is covered in Herodotus Book 8, and the Athenian expedition to Sicily in Thucydides Books 6 and 7. Insights into Roman cooks and cooking may be found in Plautus: *Rudens, Miles Gloriosus, Aulularia* and *Pseudolus*; and there are splendid 'parasites' in Plautus' *Captivi* and Terence's *The Eunuch*. Juvenal (especially Satires 3 and 9) may be plundered for accounts of strange dinner-party customs. Horace's *Epistles* and Pliny's *Letters* contain much about Roman attitudes to the country, and the pleasures of the simple life.

FOLLOW-UP ACTIVITIES

1 Make a map of the Greek and Roman world. Show the kind of produce found in each area, and the main sources of imports. Use a classical atlas to help you with the detail. (Chapter 1)

2 List the foods and cooking utensils in your own home. Next to them, put Greek or Roman alternatives where they exist. Which are special to the ancient world, and which to us? (Chapters 1 and 7)

3 Imagine you are a Greek host, inviting friends for a dinner-party and *symposion*. Write a letter telling them what food and entertainment you hope to provide. (Chapters 2 and 4)

4 What would you store in the larder of a Greek house, and how would you organise the storage? Write instructions like those in the extract on page 19. (Chapter 2)

5 Choose a single dish or complete meal. Give the class a talk on how it should be prepared and served (Chapters 2, 5, 6, 7)

6 Draw a scene of Greek farmers, merchant ships or soldiers. Use Greek pictures to make your people and ships as accurate as possible. (Chapter 3)

7 Read the account of Artemon's and Apollodoros' trading fraud. Imagine you are helping them plan their next trip. Write to them explaining the scheme you have in mind. (Chapter 3)

8 Read some of Homer's *Iliad*, or arrange a playreading or cassette recording of Aristophanes' *Acharnians* with some friends. (Chapter 3)

9 Draw or paint a scene from a *symposion* or *comissatio*: host, guests, slaves, entertainers. Use pictures to make your people as accurate as you can. (Chapters 4 and 6)

10 Imagine you are a newspaper reporter at the court of King Nestor. Write a report for your paper, with pictures, of his thanksgiving sacrifice. (Chapter 4)

11 Imagine you are a Greek boy or girl, preparing for your wedding. Write down or give a talk about the events planned for the day, and the menus. (Chapter 4)

12 Organise a class debate on the motion 'This house would rather eat to live than live to eat'. (Chapter 5)

13 Make up a week's menus for a Roman household: father, mother, two children and three slaves. (Chapter 5)

14 Find out all you can about Roman farming, and the way the slaves were treated. Cato and Varro are the best authors to read. (Chapter 5)

15 Read 'Trimalchio's Dinner-party'. Improvise the conversation of some of the guests, and write it or record it as a play. (Chapter 6)

16 Draw or model the zodiac dish from 'Trimalchio's Dinner-party'. What modern foods would you put on each sign on a zodiac dish? (Chapter 6)

17 Try some of the recipes given. (If you cannot get some of the ingredients, use modern alternatives.) If the dish works, try it on your family, friends and teachers. (Chapter 7)

General Topics

18 Imagine you are an ancient Greek or Roman, time-travelling in twentieth-century Britain. Write an entry for your journal describing how you reacted to visiting a modern kitchen, and watching the natives eat a meal.
19 Find out about wine-making in Greece and Rome. Where – and how – were the best grapes grown? How were they processed? How was the wine marketed?
20 Find out about the water supply in Greek and Roman towns. Where did the water come from? How was it delivered to the town? How did it get to the people? What happened to the water supply in a siege?